T0013844

Life in Numbers

Smart Shoppers

Karin Anderson, M.A.T.

Publishing Credits

Rachelle Cracchiolo, M.S.Ed., *Publisher*
Conni Medina, M.A.Ed., *Managing Editor*
Nika Fabienke, Ed.D., *Series Developer*
June Kikuchi, *Content Director*
John Leach, *Assistant Editor*
Kevin Pham, *Graphic Designer*

TIME For Kids and the TIME For Kids logo are registered trademarks of TIME Inc. Used under license.

Image Credits: front cover, p.1 Tooykrub/Shutterstock; p.16 jfmdesign/ iStock; p.23 second from top: Kunal Mehta/Shutterstock.com; all other images from iStock and/or Shutterstock.

Teacher Created Materials
5301 Oceanus Drive
Huntington Beach, CA 92649-1030
http://www.tcmpub.com
ISBN 978-1-4258-4956-6

We shop at a grocery store! We choose what to buy.

We need a cart.
Should we get a
small **basket** or a
big cart?

I choose the big cart.

We need fruit. Mom asks, "Should we buy apples or pears?"

I choose both.
We buy three
apples and five
pears.

We need carrots. "Should we buy big or small carrots?" asks Mom.

I choose eight
small carrots.

We need eggs.
Here are twelve
eggs.

Here are six eggs. We choose twelve eggs.

We have money
left for one treat!

I choose ice cream!

We had fun
shopping.

We made many choices.

Glossary

basket

choices

grocery store

shopping